DINOSAUR TIME

An EARLY I CAN READ Book®

E
X 568,19

BY PEGGY PARISH
PICTURES BY ARNOLD LOBEL

Harper & Row, Publishers
New York, Evanston, San Francisco, London

for Betsy and Rob Reid—
with love

Early I Can Read Book is a registered trademark
of Harper & Row, Publishers, Inc.

DINOSAUR TIME
Text copyright © 1974 by Margaret Parish
Illustrations copyright © 1974 by Arnold Lobel

Library of Congress Catalog Card Number: 73–14331
Trade Standard Book Number: 06–024653–7
Harpercrest Standard Book Number: 06–024654–5

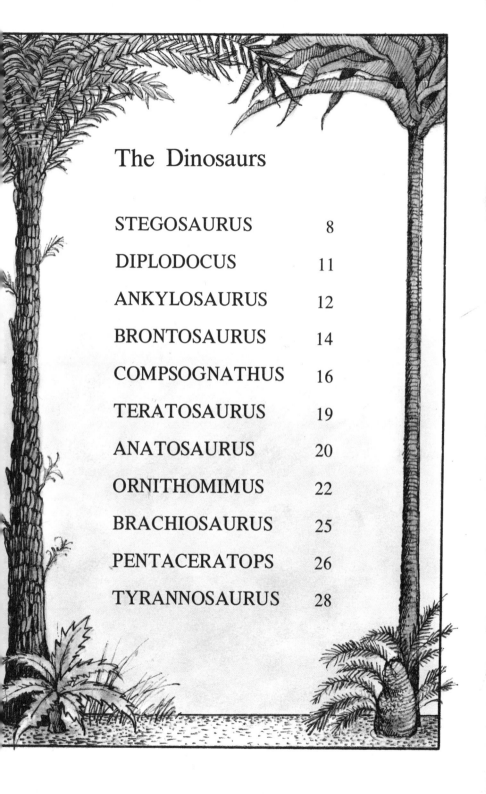

The Dinosaurs

Long, long ago

the world was different.

More land was under water.

It was warm all the time.

And dinosaurs

were everywhere. . . .

There were big dinosaurs.

There were small ones.

There were fast dinosaurs, and slow ones.

Some dinosaurs ate meat.

Some ate plants.

STEGOSAURUS

This is how you say it—

steg-uh-SAW-russ

This dinosaur

had plates on its back.

They were made of bone.

It had sharp points

on its tail.

It ate plants.

Its name is Stegosaurus.

DIPLODOCUS

This is how you say it—

dip-LAH-duh-cuss

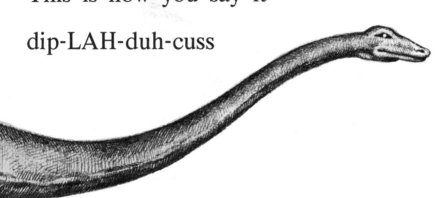

This dinosaur was long.

But most of it was neck and tail.

Its teeth were short and dull.

It ate plants.

Its name is Diplodocus.

ANKYLOSAURUS

This is how you say it—

ank-eye-loh-SAW-russ

This dinosaur
had a shell like a turtle.
Its tail was like a club.
Not many animals
could hurt it.
Its name is Ankylosaurus.

BRONTOSAURUS

This is how you say it—

bron-tuh-SAW-russ

This dinosaur
was a giant.
But its mouth was tiny.
It ate plants.
It ate, and ate, and ate
to fill up its big body.
Its name is Brontosaurus.

COMPSOGNATHUS

This is how you say it—

comp-sog-NAYTH-uss

This dinosaur

was small.

It was as big as a cat.

But it could run fast.

It could catch other animals

and eat them.

Its name is Compsognathus.

TERATOSAURUS

This is how you say it—

tare-at-oh-SAW-russ

This dinosaur

walked on its back legs.

It had big claws,

and sharp teeth.

It ate meat.

Its name is Teratosaurus.

ANATOSAURUS

This is how you say it—

an-at-oh-SAW-russ

This dinosaur

is called a "duckbill."

It had a beak like a duck.

Its beak had no teeth.

But its mouth did.

There were hundreds

of teeth in it!

Sometimes a tooth broke.

But that did not matter.

It could grow a new one.

Its name is Anatosaurus.

ORNITHOMIMUS

This is how you say it—

or-nith-oh-MY-muss

This dinosaur had a beak, too.

But it had no teeth.

It ate small animals and insects.

Maybe it ate fruits

and dinosaur eggs, too.

But it had no teeth.

How did it eat?

A bird eats.

It has no teeth.

Maybe it ate

like a bird.

Its name is

Ornithomimus.

BRACHIOSAURUS

This is how you say it—

brack-ee-oh-SAW-russ

This dinosaur was fat.

It was too fat

to run from enemies.

That is why it stayed in the water.

It was safe there,

and food was close by.

It ate plants.

Its name is Brachiosaurus.

PENTACERATOPS

This is how you say it—

pen-tuh-SARE-ah-tops

This dinosaur had five horns.

They were all on its face.

Its name is Pentaceratops.

This name is just right.

It means "five-horns-on-the-face."

TYRANNOSAURUS

This is how you say it—

tih-ran-uh-SAW-russ

This dinosaur

was the biggest meat-eater.

Its jaws were huge.

Its teeth were six inches long.

It ate other dinosaurs.

Its name is Tyrannosaurus.

29

Dinosaurs lived everywhere
for a long time.
Then they died.
Nobody knows why.
But once it was their world.
It was dinosaur time.

Author's Note

We do not know much about dinosaurs. No one ever saw a dinosaur.

But people have found dinosaur fossils, such as footprints, bones, and teeth. Scientists study them, and can tell how big the dinosaurs were, what they ate, and other things about the way they lived.

Scientists learn more each year. But we may never know all about dinosaurs.